A car is a significant purchase. It requires thought, research, and test drives. It's not typically something you run out and buy quickly; instead, you'll want to look under the hood and check the tires. You want to make sure you are purchasing the right vehicle for you, ensuring it has key features critical to its functioning and your safety and comfort.

Just as painstakingly as you select a car, you and your organization need to take similar care and considered measures when selecting a learning management system. An LMS is more than just a place for staff to review and complete training—it is the cornerstone of an organization's online training and development strategy. A great LMS needs to be both robust and agile enough to shift with the organization. It should not hinder progress.

In this issue of TD at Work, I will take you through the process of strategically selecting an LMS. You will learn:
- what an LMS is capable of, including the reports you can run
- who should be on the LMS selection committee
- how to create a request for information
- the most important features that should come built into your LMS
- the type of support you should expect from your LMS supplier.

You will also learn tips and tricks on how to engage your learners with the LMS and dos and don'ts around compliance training, which is often the reason an organization purchases an LMS. So, let's dive into the process and get you test-driving an LMS.

WHAT IS AN LMS AND DO YOU NEED ONE?

Before I discuss the LMS selection committee, strategy, and other aspects of this process, it's important that you understand some key terminology. Let's start with the LMS. While many talent development professionals understand the fundamentals of an LMS, not everyone is clear on exactly what it can do.

An LMS is a software application used for tracking and distributing online training. Having a well-built LMS is beneficial for both the organization and the learners. How? For starters, an LMS enables an organization to hold employees accountable for training completion. This feature is valuable for organizations that conduct a lot of compliance training, because the LMS will encapsulate training completion reports that the organization can send to regulatory bodies to prove compliance with the law. Further, the organization can send these same reports to managers to help drive training completion—that is, to let managers know which direct reports have and have not taken the required course or courses.

Likewise, employees can pull their own training completion certificates from the LMS to prove compliance achievement or organization-specific required training, such as that around onboarding or technological skills. Depending on the content within the LMS, employees can map out a pathway for their own professional development and, during performance review time, show proof of that initiative and those accomplishments.

Despite the benefits of an LMS to many organizations for varying reasons, the system comes at a great expense. The contract with a supplier is normally three years, with the dollar amount calculated by the number of employees accessing the LMS. Even for a company with 4,000 employees, the LMS can be a $60,000 budget line item for the L&D team. An expense that large could be hard for many training departments to rationalize and incur.

Think about it this way: The cost of the LMS, in some cases, would be same as the annual salary for one full-time employee. If you are seriously considering purchasing an LMS, you must determine where in your talent development strategy the LMS fits.

Review this list of questions to help you determine whether your company needs an LMS. If you answer yes to a question, add a detailed response as to why.
- Do you have any regulatory training that requires monitoring or consistent completion?
- Do your company goals require tracking and reporting on individual course completions for promotions, goal progress, or return on investment calculation?
- Is your organization looking to cut travel expenses by creating more e-learning opportunities or hosting more webinars?
- Does your online learning strategy include self-paced learning opportunities?
- Do you have the resources on your current team to implement and administer an LMS?
- Do you currently do anything that can be considered online learning?

Tally your responses. If you answered yes no more than three times, your organization probably doesn't need an LMS. For those who answered yes primarily, understand that your online learning strategy drives your LMS selection. Your next step is to develop this strategy, which needs to be in place before you select an LMS.

Know Your Options

Learn your learning management system vocabulary, because there are numerous LMS options.

Name	Description	Supplier
MOOC	MOOC stands for massive open online courses. Depending on the size of your organization, using a MOOC for staff development can be a cheaper alternative to purchasing an LMS. It will also save the talent development team the time of building and uploading content.	Lynda.com Coursera Udemy
Off-the-Shelf	These systems come with built-in content or are created by course-authoring software and content suppliers.	CourseMill Docebo Articulate Online
Open Source	This is a free, web-based LMS.	Moodle ATutor Eliademy
Enterprise	This is a traditional LMS that you and your organization must populate with content after implementation.	Skillsoft Cornerstone SumTotal

DEVELOPING AN ONLINE LEARNING STRATEGY

To establish your online learning strategy, ask yourself some key questions, including:
- Do we currently do anything that can be considered online learning? If not, why do we want to start online learning (such as to save travel expenses or because new regulations are leading to compliance requirements)?
- What are the short- and long-term goals for our online learning program?
- What does success of our online learning program look like?
- Are we considering creating content that will be sold? Will we, for example, have some content to provide externally in addition to what we offer internally? If so, what will this external-focused content look like? How much will we charge for those materials? (Note: If you charge for content, you will need an LMS that can support payment.)
- What do you envision as the LMS's overall purpose?

Last, you will want to make a decision about integration. What systems will integrate into the LMS and why? For example, will your organization want to integrate an HR system (such as a human resource information system or management system) into the LMS? Will you want to connect outside learning plans, such as LinkedIn Learning, to your LMS? Start this conversation with the appropriate individuals as a part of the organization's overall online learning strategy. This should not be a last-minute decision.

After you have answered these questions, decide whether your organization needs an LMS to successfully achieve your online learning strategy. If not, then you don't need an LMS.

If an LMS will help you achieve success, use your answers to develop the online learning strategy and goals for your LMS. Make sure your online learning goals follow the SMART (specific, measurable, achievable, relevant, and time-bound) format so that they are concrete and make business sense to your organization.

For example, your goals may read along these lines:
Specific. We will use our LMS to house the record of completion for all new hires' compliance training.
Measurable. Compliance training will open every October and close every January 31.
Achievable. All new hires will receive a login to the LMS during new hire orientation, so they are able to complete training.

Relevant. XYZ compliance training is now required and will be reviewed during all HR audits.

Time-Bound. The LMS administrator will provide completion reports on a daily, weekly, and monthly basis during the compliance training window.

Your goal statement, built on SMART goals, may read: "All new hires will access the LMS to complete the required new hire compliance training between October 1 and January 31. This training program is now required and will be reviewed during all HR audits. The LMS administrator will run reports on a daily, weekly, and monthly basis during the compliance window."

If you decide that an LMS would greatly augment your online strategy—that is, that you conduct a lot of compliance training that requires monitoring, report individual courses for the purpose of promotion, have self-paced learning options that you are interested in keeping track of, and have a considerable amount of training assets as online courses—it's time to move ahead and assemble a team that will help you decide what you need from your LMS and who can help fulfill those needs.

THE LMS TEAM

Now that you've decided to purchase an LMS, here's a fact to keep in mind to help you and your organization avoid a common mistake: Most LMS implementations fail because the group selecting the LMS is not the group using the LMS, so your team is crucial.

Selecting the Team

When putting together your LMS selection committee, make sure to build this from a cross-section of LMS users and other relevant stakeholders, including:

Members from the talent development team. These individuals will be creating the content and potentially paying the bill. This group will also fully develop the online learning strategy.

The LMS administrator. This individual will be tasked with working with the supplier, uploading content into the LMS, and running reports. (I delve into this role further below.)

HR. An individual from HR will help ensure that the LMS can provide all the necessary regulatory reports. This individual—and her team—will also be beneficial for any HR-related system integrations and in helping determine whether employee training completed at home will qualify as billable hours.

Integration With Other HR Systems

As part of developing the online learning strategy, you will want to determine whether other HR systems will be integrated into the LMS. If your strategy is to use the LMS for performance reviews or other HR-only related tasks, then the LMS must be able to integrate with these systems. And you and the selection committee will need to bring up your integration needs during every LMS supplier demo. If possible, ask for a demo of how the integration process works from end to end within the LMS.

Because integration is such a thorny issue, it may be helpful to consider using an out-of-the-box LMS that one of your HR suppliers offers. Not every HR system has an LMS, but if so, the upside is that the systems are already designed to work together. If you're using the LMS solely for HR-related items, this may be the best option to limit frustration and confusion when attempting to integrate the two systems.

IT. An IT staffer needs to be involved from the beginning. This individual will understand the constraints of your organization's technology and know whether you can even support adding an LMS. Further, it's critical to consider potential data breaches. IT will want to test or understand such things as the LMS's vulnerability to hacking.

A variety of end users. What expectations do you have for your end users with the LMS and even for online learning at the organization more broadly? Will they be able to use their phone or mobile device for training? If so, this changes the types of LMS suppliers you will consider. Do users need to be able to pull their own reports? What reports will they look for? These questions can dramatically change the supplier that you will end up selecting. If you don't provide content in the format your users can access or that you or they desire and make sure the user interface is user-friendly, no one will fully use the LMS.

Makeup of a Learning Management System Administrator

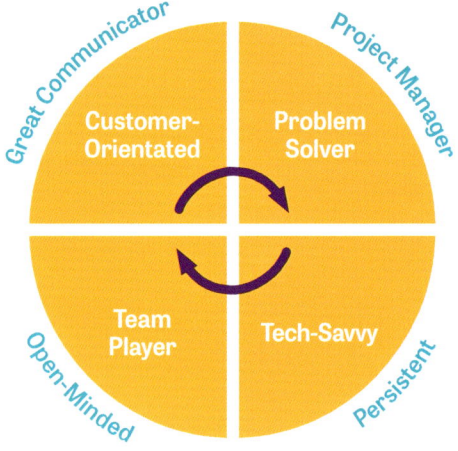

Duties	
Course Administration	**Reporting**
Creating courses, uploading content, verifying course completions	Generating and communication
Site Administration	**User Management**
Creating front page copy, course descriptions, managing all site-wide default settings	Configuring roles and permissions, Tier I–Tier III troubleshooting, managing site access

Skills
Strategic thinker • E-learning course development • Copywriter • MS Office suite • Adobe suite

Working With the LMS Administrator

As noted above, the LMS administrator has a critical role on the LMS team. This individual will be integral to successfully selecting and implementing your LMS. If your organization is selecting an LMS for the first time and you have the advantage of helping select the administrator, look for an individual who has project management skills, is a great communicator, and who is persistent yet open-minded. You will work closely with this individual to carry out the online learning strategy and periodically re-evaluate the LMS and supplier.

The administrator will also be the main point of contact with the LMS supplier you select and must maintain strong relationships. Finally, the administrator will work closely with employees across the organization in carrying out such duties as course administration and site administration.

If you are unable to help select the LMS administrator, see the sidebar above about the necessary skills and knowledge an LMS administrator should have. This will help you realize and appreciate all that the administrator is bringing to the table.

MUST-HAVE LMS FEATURES

Once you have formed the selection committee, start the group brainstorming expectations for our organization's LMS. The group should also survey individuals outside the committee to learn their expectations. But before the selection committee can make a list of what it wants out of the LMS, it needs to understand what is and isn't possible. Let's look at the core features you'll want to look for in an LMS.

Remember that purchasing an LMS is a significant investment. A car isn't complete without a first-class engine, and that's how you should view the features that come built into an LMS. Don't get confused or enticed by all the bells and whistles that you may hear about. Rather, look at the major requirements.

These are the features your LMS must have.

Intuitive Design (and Not Just for the End User)

Some LMSs may have an impressive administration site but a clunky end user experience. On the other hand, other LMSs have a great design for the end user, but the administrative side is so painful that the LMS administrator will be unable to navigate the site.

In my previous roles as the LMS administrator, I lived on the LMS administration site. I launched it the minute I walked into work and only closed it when I left for the day. A great LMS should have a design that works for both the admin and the end users. The administrator will have other responsibilities than managing the site, so she can't afford to waste precious time on a less-than-accessible site. Meanwhile, end users are going to drag their feet if the site is difficult for them to use. The organization may get the end user to complete the required compliance programs, but employees certainly won't go out of their way to enroll in voluntary professional development if the LMS is a challenge to use.

Robust and Easy Reporting

Proof of training completion is one of the main reasons companies purchase an LMS. These completion reports are essential—sometimes because of regulatory requirements and other times for performance proof.

LMS reports will primarily fall into three categories:
- **Course completion.** Use these reports to monitor each user's completion; in most cases, the reports provide the completion date and time.
- **User maintenance.** If offered, reports in this category provide information about the number of logins at both the organizational and individual levels.
- **Site administration.** Use these reports to measure the most and least popular courses. This is an important report category, although some suppliers may not offer site administration or user maintenance reports.

Here are some facets to consider around the reporting element of an LMS.

Dashboards should come prebuilt, but they should also be customizable by an administrator or manager. Having dashboards set up in advance will enable managers to monitor their staff's and their own training completion. This will help limit the amount of reports being requested from your LMS administrator or talent development team.

Real-time training completion reports are must-haves. Even the smallest delay can cause confusion and frustration. If the potential supplier has a delay in training completion report updates, this must be communicated to all parties. This is especially critical during compliance time when reports are being sent multiple times per day or week to managers and senior executives.

Intuitive and clean reports are also critical. A new administrator or manager should be able to understand how to run a report at first glance. The final output should be easy to read and interpret. If it takes more than three steps to run a report, move to the next supplier.

You may not be able to determine the number of steps to run a report in the request for information (see the next section for more on RFIs), but during demos with prospective suppliers, the selection committee can request to see all the report options and even ask to see how to generate them. Three steps may seem overly simple, but stop and think through them. In any LMS you choose, you'll want to be able to:
- quickly navigate to the reports area
- open a prebuilt template
- click to run the report.

> A great LMS should have a design that works for both the admin and the end users.

More steps are likely a hinderance to running reports. And that means your LMS administrator will always be tasked with running reports rather than being free to work with the talent development or training director to build the online learning strategy.

Powerful Built-In Exam Tools

Yes, you can build an exam into your course-authoring software. But using these types of exams can become a burden to your LMS administrator and end users. The exam tool inside the LMS should enable the end user to test out of a course at least once. This feature is important for companies that conduct annual training. The same tool should also allow for multiple and limited numbers of exam retakes. Your course-authoring software may already have all these capabilities, but using that rather than the LMS to make these types of decisions can make course design difficult, because it is cumbersome to build those features in the course authoring software.

Another great reason to have exam tools built into the LMS is that they make updating exam questions easier. The LMS administrator can run exam completion reports and see which exam questions are commonly answered incorrectly. That information could be helpful to course developers in determining whether the course needs updates. This information can also be helpful to managers for performance reviews in establishing what areas their staff need additional support. You can't receive this level of detail when the exam is built inside course-authoring software.

Intuitive Course Upload and Retirement

Retiring a course within the LMS should be something that your LMS administrator can do in one click. Uploading a course should likewise be easy. Unless you are doing uploads and retirements en masse, you should not need to contact the supplier for this task—but in those instances, you should be able to ask your supplier for assistance.

During the demos, ask the suppliers to tell the selection committee how their other clients handle uploading and retiring courses. You may learn that other clients contact the supplier for this task in all instances, which could be another element that your LMS administrator doesn't have to do.

Auto-Enrollment

Your LMS administrator should not be expected to spend all her time manually enrolling people into courses. During the selection and design process, the selection committee is right to expect that all courses for new hires are auto-assigned when their account is created in the LMS. If this is not something you can do in the LMS, look for another supplier. The overall design of everything within the LMS—from the way users are added to the way the courses are loaded—should be designed so that an administrator does not manually assign anything.

The LMS administrator should be free to work on growing usage, making site improvements, and site adoption. Your LMS administrator can't do these things if she is always assigning courses.

Flexibility in the Overall Design

Flexibility is not as much a specific feature as it is an overall manner of being. A company's mission and vision can change quickly and unexpectedly. Thus, your LMS should be able to quickly adapt to changes in business without supplier help all the time. Some work the supplier will have to do, but your LMS administrator should be able to handle simple tasks like loading course thumbnail images.

Be sure to think about this if your team doesn't have the resources to administer the LMS—what options can be built into your contract so that the supplier is responsible for making small and large changes within the LMS.

Robust Library of Content

Sometimes finding an LMS supplier that has a library of great content and a well-built LMS is difficult. But if you can find it—and the LMS has the other features we've discussed—it's a win-win. Employees want to learn, and if you use learning as an engagement tool, you will see your employees flourish in ways you never imagined.

If your organization is only looking for an LMS for professional development, consider an off-the-shelf system. An off-the-shelf LMS comes with built-in content. This is beneficial for a few reasons:

- End users can access a large library of training courses.
- Managers can work with employees to set expectations for self-paced learning.
- Return on investment for the expense is easily calculated by using a variety of training completion reports.

Content is king. And this case is no different. Your new or updated LMS needs to have content that meets all your end users' needs.

Be sure that while developing your online learning strategy that you have established the content you'll need. Some examples of content worth purchasing off the shelf are leadership training; modules that enhance or extend your current compliance training; and basic professional development, such as courses on MS Office, time management, project management, and how to run a meeting. Regardless of how the modules are added into the LMS, a library of content is necessary.

DEVELOPING A REQUEST FOR INFORMATION

Now that the selection committee understands the must-have aspects of an LMS, members should agree on the features that their LMS should be equipped with and then create an RFI, which the committee will send to LMS suppliers to let them know that your organization is in the market for an LMS.

An RFI is meant to collect information about potential suppliers and what each has to offer. Each supplier will have strengths and weaknesses, and it's critical to use this information to help meet your company's needs. Although it may take time to create the RFI, it is a worthwhile endeavor.

Choosing an Open Source LMS

How do you know whether your organization should choose an open source learning management system rather than a traditional option? An open source LMS may be a good option for a company that lacks the budget to pay for a traditional system.

There are certainly quality open source LMS options, such as Moodle. The platform features several of the top LMS requirements, including dashboards to monitor course completion, a variety of course completion reports, and responsive support from an online community of users. Moodle also offers prebuilt options to enable users to create mobile-ready courses. Because it is a popular open source LMS, it has a large online support community, through which organizations can get answers to questions almost immediately as well as download premade e-learning courses and templates.

However, because open source LMSs are free, you lose the one-on-one contact and support that you would receive with a traditional LMS supplier. Further, as you consider an open source LMS, you'll want to verify whether it can grow and shift with your business needs, which likely it won't. So, if your organization is selecting an open source option, it is critical that you have detailed, well-thought-out, and SMART goals for the LMS.

Ultimately, as I've reiterated throughout this issue, choosing the right LMS for your organization comes down to your online learning strategy and where the LMS fits into that picture.

The committee can use the RFI to determine the budget, implementation timeframe, and functionality of different LMSs. The RFI should precede the request for proposals (RFP), which is meant to promote bidding from different LMS suppliers.

Eventually, the committee will score all RFI responses and use these to either create a short list of suppliers from which to see a demonstration or to serve as the basis for the RFP. *Note*: You are not required to create an RFI; however, using one will bring suppliers to your door versus you having to seek them out.

Further, you do not need a long RFI, but it should include:
- Key points from your online learning strategy, such as your purpose for the LMS, the business need or goal that the LMS will support, and how many employees will be accessing the system.
- The LMS features you are looking for, such as a list of the types of reports you will want to run and who (the administrator or end users, for example) can access them.
- A list of references or examples of work from previous implementations.
- Information about what supplier support should look like (such as whether you desire 24/7 customer service and who the point of contact is).

CHOOSING AND WORKING WITH A SUPPLIER

Because an LMS is a significant expense for an organization to take on, you need an LMS supplier that is responsive and customer centric. If you don't have support when you or your end users need it, no one will use the LMS and your company will have wasted resources, something it can't afford.

As you review supplier contracts, consider their response time as well as your control and upgrade options.

Supplier Response Time

The supplier's contract must outline what support, including response time, will look like.

Monthly check-in calls between the supplier, LMS administrator, and talent development or training director are vital to the health of your LMS. Your LMS administrator and supplier's account representative should be on a first-name basis. There should be nothing that happens in your LMS that your account representative isn't aware of and vice versa. The in-house organizational team supporting the LMS should have full transparency from the supplier about any bugs, patches, and required upgrades.

Email response time of no more than 48 hours is key. Your LMS will be open 24/7, 365 days a year. The supplier help desk should have similar hours. It is important that the selection committee complete due diligence on the front end. The supplier isn't going to tell you it has

Components of a Request for Information

A well-crafted request for information (RFI) lets suppliers know that your organization is serious about the learning management system purchase and that they should compete for your business. Here are the typical components of an RFI that you can use as the foundation for building yours. Work with the selection committee to identify your desires for each component.

Introduction
Briefly state some general information about your organization and the purpose of the RFI. Provide details regarding to whom suppliers should direct questions about the RFI.

Objective
Provide basic context of your needs. A supplier should be able to quickly review this section and determine immediately if their offering is right for your organization.

Response Instructions
Give any instructions related to suppliers completing and submitting the RFI, such as the deadline and point of contact.

Response Format
Provide basic instructions on the RFI format you desire, such as a cover page, overview of the supplier, list of current clients, or page limit. Determine what will make reviewing responses easiest. For example, I recommend asking for a table of contents so you can go directly to the information you want to review.

    Note: You have the option to include a template. If you do, make sure to indicate where suppliers can find the template in the RFI.

Demo Request
State that only selected suppliers will be invited to demo, and detail how you will conduct the demos, such as in person or via webinar.

Timeline
Include the timeline that the selection committee has developed, including the submission deadline, length of time the selection committee will spend reviewing and scoring responses, demo invitation date, and date for demo day. State that dates may change and that this timeline is a guideline. This section is also about transparency and holds the selection committee accountable for the review process.

Rules
Stipulate that an RFI submission does not obligate you to purchasing a supplier's solution. If your legal department has standard wording, use that language. If not, work with someone with legal expertise to craft a statement that protects your organization's interests.

RFI Topics of Interest
Use this section to ask suppliers questions related to the various aspects of the LMS you are looking for. This will help you understand what each supplier is able to deliver. Group the questions around individual areas of interest, such as enterprise-level solution and scalability, security and authentication, features, testing, course reporting, mobile access, client support, and pricing.

poor response time, but someone in your network will. This is one reason it is critical to ask each supplier for references and a list of clients.

The response time is one aspect that should be built into your contract. This way, when you call the supplier, it is aware it has 48 hours to respond to your company.

A customer support line, where an individual answers the phone, is vital to the success of your implementation and the efficacy of your LMS. The contract should also outline what escalation looks like when the help desk is unavailable.

Upgrade and Version Control

This may seem small, but you want to be able to upgrade your LMS when you want—not when the supplier tells you it's time and convenient on its end. The upgrade could be small changes—a tweak or a patch to replace a bug—or large, substantial changes. Either way, make sure that you have dedicated staff to communicate the change to end users.

Another consideration is whether you will receive a free upgrade. With the right account or sales representative, this may not be something you need to worry about; however, with the wrong rep, this could become an issue.

Be sure to get everything in writing. What you feel is a strong relationship with an account rep may change if your point of contact leaves the supplier. Remember that, just as you expect your talent to continue to grow and develop new skills, your LMS is expected to grow with the organization. You need to understand any hinderance to growth on the supplier's part and have this documented within your contract.

> Your LMS will be open 24/7, 365 days a year. The supplier help desk should have similar hours.

Your signed contract should specifically outline the roles of potentially two different individuals: your account representative and your sales representative. This will depend on your supplier as to whether two individuals fill these two roles. You will want outlined the level of involvement these people have with your LMS. For example, whom should you contact with Level 1 support questions? This could be your representative and not the supplier help desk. This type of information is important to know.

Another question to raise either ahead of the supplier demo or certainly at that time are responsibilities regarding general and advanced site maintenance. Who has the right to make changes in the system? Are some things locked down to only the supplier? If so, what are those things? The supplier should provide a document that explains this information quickly and concisely.

TIPS FOR USING THE LMS

We've covered how to select an LMS and the features you should require in the system, whether you choose an open source solution, out-of-the-box system, or a traditional LMS.

Demo Day

A demo should be a requirement of your selection process and stated within your request for information. During the demos, the selection committee (or other individuals included in the demo day process) will be able to view all the features of the supplier's LMS and ask questions and request additional information. Demos can also be opportunities for selection committee members to learn how to run reports.

If the rep can't answer your questions, respectfully ask him to provide you with a resource who can better assist you. During the demos, each committee member should have a selection tool (see the job aid at the end of this issue for an example). Having this tool handy will make it easier for everyone to later share opinions on each supplier without trying to recall from memory answers to questions and overall impressions. Questions to ask and items to consider include end user and administrative navigation, ease of integration, and ease of uploading and retiring courses.

But with everything in training and talent development, the employee matters most. If they aren't using the content—either because of a clunky interface or because the material doesn't meet their learning needs or isn't engaging—you're not getting your money's worth or being successful.

So, how can you ensure that employees use the LMS, and how can you use the system that you may have spent considerable resources on to go beyond learning and improve the organizational culture?

Increase Utilization

There is no point in having an LMS that no one uses unless directed. Here are a few tips on how to pull learners to your LMS:

- During implementation, make sure champions are hyping up the LMS. These may be end users who served as part of the selection committee or senior leaders whose support you sought in purchasing or bringing the LMS onboard.
- Gamify your language, such as asking "How many course badges did you collect?" People play games because they're fun, because they serve as practice, for social bonding reasons, and the list goes on. When you frame the LMS in terms of games, you tap a deep human psychological need.
- Empower managers to run their own completion reports. This autonomy is a win-win: It saves the LMS administrator time as well as the manager, who doesn't need to ask for the information and wait until the administrator has the opportunity to respond.
- Host a virtual open house for the LMS at least once a quarter. Give managers and employees a chance to learn, starting with how to use the LMS and seeing all that it has to offer.

Build Employee Engagement

If your organization suffers from low employee engagement, providing learning opportunities is a great way to change that. This is not a requirement when deciding to purchase an LMS, but some LMS suppliers provide systems that you can use to track both training completion and performance. If your organization is thinking about that kind of LMS (based on your online learning strategy), here are some suggestions on how to better engage your staff and drive adoption of the new system.

- Complete all onboarding tasks within the LMS. This would include all new-hire training, if applicable;

Case Study: Dollar Tree

Implementing your new learning management system requires a coordinated effort—and that's just what Dollar Tree did with iLearn, the internal name of its LMS. These are the steps the talent development team took:

- It engaged senior leadership in marketing initiatives by using video blogs to show support for online learning. Dollar Tree uploaded these blogs to the LMS and used them as an integral part of new-hire orientation to connect new employees with the company.
- It partnered with its suppliers—core services, solution services, and the custom development team—to secure help executing the online learning strategy. Some training content was built in-house, but Dollar Tree purchased other content from the supplier to build a robust training library before going live.
- It capitalized on the supplier's robust library of content to develop a top-notch leadership development program. Building the next generation of leaders is an element of Dollar Tree's strategy, so having this content preloaded into the LMS enabled the talent development team to close a gap in its training program.

Dollar Tree's talent development team was able to take these steps because it first spent the time to develop an online learning strategy and then selected a supplier that could meet all the organization's needs. The supplier was responsive and is able to grow with the organization. Heather McCoy, manager of Dollar Tree's learning technology, describes the supplier as a partner. "When our organization has a business need, I can pick up the phone and speak with our client representative about that need."

new-hire paperwork; and performance reviews. This develops an early mindset with employees that the LMS is a go-to resource.
- Create a newsletter for the LMS that showcases the most completed courses, users with the most completed courses, and recently uploaded or updated courses. Distribute the newsletter to the entire organization to generate healthy competition and interest in new courses and to showcase all the self-paced learning available to staff.
- Create space and time for accessing the LMS to learn something new. My favorite is called 5 @ 5. Invite learners to log in at 5 p.m. and spend at least five minutes learning something new.
- Use lunch & learns to share knowledge across the organization. Where do employees sign up to attend the event? The LMS, of course.
- Create monthly themes around key topics and center all learning around that topic. For example, compliance isn't a once-a-year training event; it's something that is required every day. Use the LMS to talk about ways everyone can be more compliant.

Annual Review of Your LMS Supplier

While this tip is geared toward you as the talent development practitioner, it can also lead to employees using the LMS more. During the performance review cycle, work with the LMS administrator and end users to complete a performance review on the LMS. Is the LMS meeting both the administrator's and end users' needs and expectations? Is the supplier responsive? Do you have the necessary content?

Use this information in later decisions to consider an LMS supplier change, advocate for using more features within the LMS, or request more funding to purchase additional content.

Note: If you are planning to ask for additional funding, do your homework before approaching senior leadership and have the necessary data on current content usage and why or how additional content would benefit the organization.

CONCLUSION

Although a large expense, an LMS is worth the investment to grow your employees and improve or prove your training completion. As with so many facets of a talent development initiative, doing the heavy lifting early in the process and making sure you include all of the relevant stakeholders will improve the odds for success. In the words of Simon Sinek, start with the "why": What purpose do you want your LMS to serve? Then follow through with the research and the effort necessary to select the right LMS for your organization and then engage end users.

REFERENCES & RESOURCES

Book
Foreman, S.D. 2017. *The LMS Guide Book*. Alexandria, VA: ATD Press.

Infoline
Lindenberg, S. 2012. "Selecting and Implementing an LMS." *Infoline*. Alexandria, VA: ASTD Press.

Online Resources
Moodle. 2018. "What is Moodle?" https://youtu.be/3ORsUGVNxGs.

Powell, M. 2017. "What is a Learning Management System?" May 17. www.docebo.com/blog/what-is-learning-management-system.

Skillsoft. 2012. "Dollar Tree Partners With Skillsoft." https://vimeo.com/46640393.

LMS Suppliers
Articulate, https://articulate.com/articulate-online

ATutor, www.atutor.ca

Cornerstone, www.cornerstoneondemand.com

Coursera, www.coursera.org

Docebo, www.docebo.com

Eliademy, https://eliademy.com

Lynda.com, www.lynda.com

Moodle, https://moodle.org

Skillsoft, www.skillsoft.com

SumTotal, www.sumtotalsystems.com

Trivantis, www.trivantis.com/products/coursemill-learning-management

Udemy, www.udemy.com

JOB AID

LMS SELECTION CHECKLIST

Purpose: Use this checklist when reviewing requests for information and during demo day to effectively score suppliers. Note: The selection committee will need to determine what score qualifies a supplier to move on to the demo phase.

Committee Member Name: _____

Department/Role (circle one):

Talent Development	HR	LMS Administrator	IT	End User

RFI Review

LMS Supplier Name: _____

Key Features: Rate the ease of use for each of the key features and total the scores. Add all committee members' total scores and place average score in the provided field.

Rate each supplier on a scale of 1–5; 1 = Does not meet expectations, 5 = Exceeds expectations.

Feature	End-user Navigation	Reporting	Uploading Content	Auto-Enrollment	Ease of Integration	Administrative Navigation	Supplier Support
Score							

Total: _____
Average Score: _____
Demo Requested (circle one): Yes   No

Demo Day

Demo Date: _____

Rate: Rate the ease of use for each of the key features and total the scores. Add all committee members' total scores and place the average score in the provided field. Calculate the final score by adding both the RFI and the demo average score.

Rate each supplier on a scale of 1–5; 1 = Does not meet expectations, 5 = Exceeds expectations.

Feature	End-user Navigation	Reporting	Uploading Content	Auto-Enrollment	Ease of Integration	Administrative Navigation	Supplier Support
Score							

Total: _____
Average Score: _____
Final Score: _____

JOB AID

REQUEST FOR INFORMATION COMPARISON TOOL

Use this tool to keep track of responses and questions that reviewers have about the requests for information. It's important to include the date you receive the RFIs so that you avoid reviewing ones that came in late. You can use information from this document during demo day, if applicable.

Reviewed By (Selection Committee Member)	LMS Supplier Name	Date Received	RFI Score	Selected for Demo (Y/N)	Date of Demo	Demo Score	Reviewer Questions

Selecting and Managing an LMS Doesn't Have to be Painful. Ready to Take the Next Step?

"Steve's book is a clear and concise resource for those navigating the complex terrain of LMSs, where seemingly small decisions can have huge impacts. I highly recommend it."

—**Peter Berking**
Senior Learning Technologist
Eduworks Corporation

THE LMS GUIDEBOOK
Learning Management Systems Demystified
Steven D. Foreman

With so many suppliers, categories, and features, finding the right learning management system can seem impossible. Take some tips from an expert so your LMS will be the perfect fit.

ISBN 13: 978-1-60728-309-6
Product Code: 111715
Released December 2017

Order at www.td.org/LMSGuidebook | Call 844.284.9351